THIS LAND CALLED AMERICA: **WISCONSIN**

CREATIVE EDUCATION

Published by Creative Education
P.O. Box 227, Mankato, Minnesota 56002
Creative Education is an imprint of The Creative Company
www.thecreativecompany.us

Design by Blue Design (www.bluedes.com)
Art direction by Rita Marshall
Book production by The Design Lab
Printed in the United States of America

Photographs by Alamy (aaron peterson.net, Arcaid, Linda Freshwaters Arndt,
Danita Delimont, Kim Karpeles, Arni Katz, North Wind Picture Archives),
AP Images (Andy Manis), Corbis (Walter Bibikow, Richard Cummins, Layne
Kennedy, Minnesota Historical Society, David Muench, Richard Hamilton
Smith, Underwood & Underwood), Getty Images (Burazin, MPI, Panoramic
Images, Ryan/Beyer), iStockphoto (Michael Thompson)

Library of Congress Cataloging-in-Publication Data
Peterson, Sheryl.
Wisconsin / by Sheryl Peterson.
p. cm. — (This land called America)
Includes bibliographical references and index.
ISBN 978-1-58341-802-4
1. Wisconsin—Juvenile literature. I. Title. II. Series.
F581.3.P48 2009
977.5—dc22   2008009532

First Edition
9 8 7 6 5 4 3 2 1

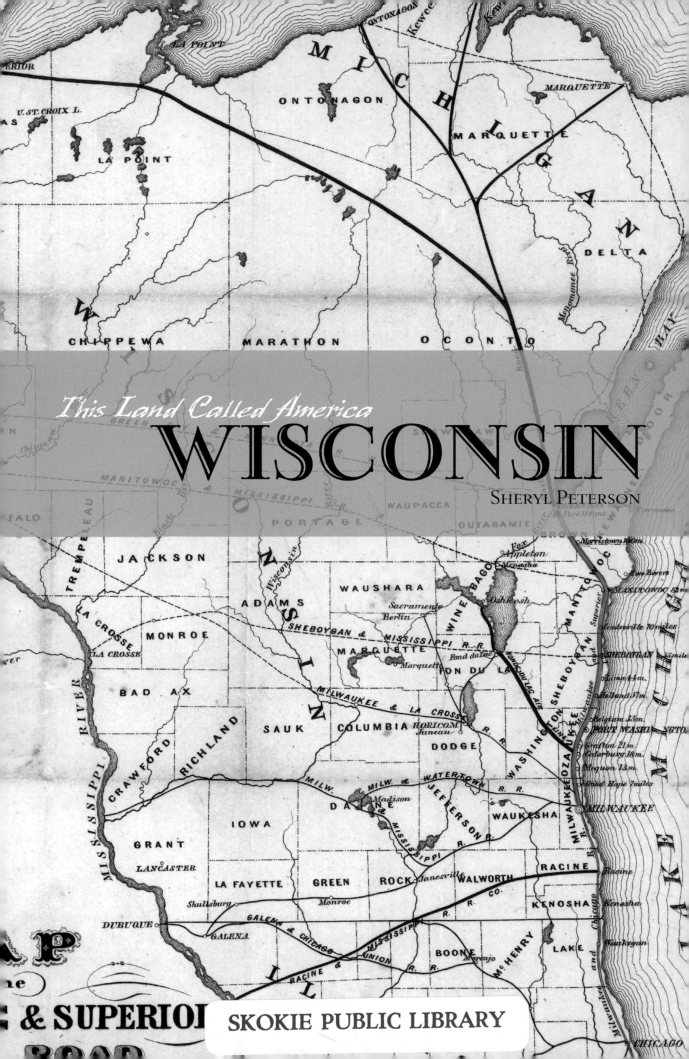

This Land Called America

WISCONSIN

Sheryl Peterson

Wisconsin

SHERYL PETERSON

IN THE FALL, WHEN THE LEAVES TURN RED AND YELLOW, PEOPLE VISIT WISCONSIN'S APPLE ORCHARDS. THE SKY IS CLEAR, AND THE AIR IS FRESH WITH THE SCENT OF APPLES. HORSE-DRAWN HAY WAGONS TAKE VISITORS ON A BUMPY RIDE TO THE APPLE GROVES. CHILDREN MUNCH CRISP APPLES WHILE THEY PICK. THEY FILL UP BAGS WITH THE ROSY, HEALTHY FRUIT. MANY ORCHARDS HAVE PUMPKINS AND RASPBERRY PATCHES, TOO. SOMETIMES ORCHARD OWNERS DEMONSTRATE HOW TO PRESS APPLES INTO SWEET CIDER. STICKY CARAMEL APPLES AND APPLE PIES ARE OFFERED FOR SALE. ON A SUNNY AUTUMN DAY, A WISCONSIN APPLE ORCHARD IS A TASTY PLACE TO BE.

YEAR
1634 French explorer Jean Nicolet discovers Lake Michigan and travels to the shores of Green Bay.
EVENT

Badger Land

In the early days, many American Indian tribes lived in Wisconsin. The Dakota settled in the forests of the northwest. The Menominee lived near rivers and lakes. They made birchbark homes and canoes. Later, the Ojibwa made their homes along Lake Superior. They harvested wild rice and hunted deer. The state's name comes from

the Ojibwa word *weeskonsan*, which means "gathering of waters."

In 1634, a French man named Jean Nicolet was the first explorer to visit the area. Nicolet canoed from Canada to the shores of Green Bay on Lake Michigan in eastern Wisconsin. Soon after, French fur traders called *voyageurs* found the forests of Wisconsin. Traders swapped blankets and kettles with the Indians for beaver pelts. French missionaries followed the traders. They taught the Indians about the Christian religion.

In 1763, England gained control of the French lands. England also ruled 13 colonies on America's East Coast. Colonists there wanted to be free. They fought against England in the Revolutionary War and won. As a result, Wisconsin became part of the new United States.

Wisconsin's native people, some of whom lived in wigwams (opposite), began meeting French traders in the 1600s (above).

YEAR
1673

EVENT
Frenchmen Jacques Marquette and Louis Joliet explore water routes from Lake Michigan to the Mississippi River.

Settlers soon entered Wisconsin from other parts of the country. Farmers came to grow corn and wheat and raise dairy cows on the flat lands of eastern Wisconsin. Warm summers were good for the crops, but the winters were long and cold.

Miners moved into the southeastern regions of Wisconsin. They dug for a rich metal called lead. Lead was used to make bullets, water pipes, and paint. Some miners did not bother to build houses. Instead, they dug tunnels and lived underground. People called them badgers. Badgers are strong, weasel-like animals that live in the ground. Later on, Wisconsin's nickname became "The Badger State."

Soon, entire families came to Wisconsin. Towns sprang up. As settlers moved in, they took over the Indians' traditional hunting grounds. Many American Indians fought to keep their land. The U.S. Army sent soldiers to protect the settlers. In 1832, a Sauk chief named Black Hawk led his people through Illinois and into Wisconsin to find new places to farm. The Army attacked and defeated the Indians in several battles during the Black Hawk War.

In times of peace, settlers began to immigrate to Wisconsin from European countries such as Germany, Norway, and Sweden. By the 1840s, the territory had more than 200,000 people. On May 29, 1848, Wisconsin became the 30th state, with Madison as its capital.

The Battle of Bad Axe, which took place near present-day Victory, Wisconsin, ended the Black Hawk War.

YEAR

1763   Wisconsin becomes part of England's colonial territories.

EVENT

The birthplace of the Republican Party is marked by an old meetinghouse in Ripon, Wisconsin.

By the 1850s, the issue of slavery divided America. Wisconsin and other Northern states did not want slavery, while the Southern states did. Anti-slavery leaders such as Horace Greeley and Salmon Chase met in Ripon in 1854. They formed the Republican Party. Abraham Lincoln joined the Republicans and was elected president in 1860. Soon after, the Civil War between the North and South began. People from Wisconsin fought for the North. The South was defeated in 1865, and slavery ended.

After the war, state businesses grew. Wisconsin led the nation in logging. Millions of trees were cut down and made into furniture and wagons. Others were used to make pulp for paper. More people moved to Wisconsin to work in the state's factories. Robert M. La Follette Sr., known as "Fighting Bob," served as Wisconsin's governor from 1901 to 1906. La Follette championed reforms for state workers. Under his leadership, Wisconsin continued to prosper.

Early lumberjacks used strong oxen to pull loads of freshly cut trees through forests.

YEAR
1832
EVENT
The Fox and Sauk Indians, led by Chief Black Hawk, are defeated, ending the Black Hawk War.

Glacial Landscape

THE MIDWESTERN STATE OF WISCONSIN IS SURROUNDED
BY FOUR STATES. MINNESOTA AND IOWA LIE TO THE WEST,
AND ILLINOIS IS TO THE SOUTH. MICHIGAN AND LAKE
SUPERIOR FORM THE NORTHERN BORDER, AND LAKE
MICHIGAN TOUCHES WISCONSIN ON THE EAST.

Huge sheets of ice called glaciers once covered Wisconsin. When the glaciers receded, they left behind deposits of rocks and debris called moraines. The glaciers also formed round craters that filled with water. These ponds are known as "kettles." The Kettle Moraine, a 100-mile (160 km) band of land on the eastern side of Wisconsin, features both kettles and moraines.

The glaciers also left thick, rich soil in the central and southern parts of Wisconsin. In central Wisconsin, prairies and hills are next to fast-flowing rivers. The Wisconsin River has carved magnificent cliffs into the landscape. Narrow passages called gorges lie between steep walls of sandstone. Farther west, tall bluffs of sandstone and limestone line the Mississippi River. Northern Wisconsin is covered with thick forests and thin, rocky soil. Loggers cut tall ash, pine, and oak trees for lumber.

Wisconsin has hundreds of waterfalls. Big Manitou Falls at Pattison State Park is the highest, at 165 feet (50 m). There are also many swift-moving trout streams and about 6,000 lakes that are large enough to be named. Lakes Mendota, Monona, Waubesa, and Kegonsa surround the capital city of Madison. The capitol itself stands between Lake Mendota and Lake Monona.

Rocky cliffs carved by glaciers tower over Devil's Lake (opposite) and over rivers in the Wisconsin Dells (above).

YEAR

1848   Wisconsin becomes the 30th state on May 29.

EVENT

T here are almost two million cows in the state. Many Wisconsinites are in the dairy business. Wisconsin produces the most milk of any state in the U.S. The state is also the top producer of butter and cheese. Two types of cheese—brick and Colby—were invented in Wisconsin.

There are more than 100,000 farms in Wisconsin. The eastern part of the state contains the best farmland. Corn is the state's leading crop. Farmers also raise soybeans and peas. Cranberries are Wisconsin's number-one fruit crop. Most of the nation's Thanksgiving cranberries come from central Wisconsin marshes. The northern city of Bayfield is famous for its apples and hosts a huge apple festival each fall.

Two of Wisconsin's most important farm products come from the state's plentiful supply of cows (above) and from its swampy cranberry bogs (opposite).

Gray wolves, the
largest wild wolves,
have steadily increased
their population in
Wisconsin recently.

Red granite, a rock made of quartz and feldspar, is mined in several spots in Wisconsin. This rock is very hard and is an excellent building material. Iron, copper, and lime are other important natural resources mined for in the state.

Although much of Wisconsin's land is used for farming or mining, the state is still heavily forested. Drivers have to be on constant watch for the many deer that live in the forests. Bears, foxes, and coyotes live in the woods, too. Even a few bobcats prowl the northern parts of the state. Fishermen catch lively trout, bass, and pike in Wisconsin waters. Ducks and geese fly over the lakes. When winter comes, the birds fly south to warmer climates.

Wisconsin winters can be harsh, as snow falls heavily throughout the state. Windstorms and blizzards move quickly across Wisconsin since there are no high mountains to slow them down. Northern parts of the state sometimes receive 100 inches (254 cm) of snow a year. Summers in Wisconsin are warm and humid.

Canada geese always fly in a V-shaped formation and rotate positions to take turns being the leader.

YEAR
1856   Educator Margarethe Schurz starts the first American kindergarten in Watertown.
EVENT

America's Dairy

THERE IS AN OLD SAYING IN WISCONSIN: "THE WORLD IS YOUR COW, BUT YOU'LL HAVE TO DO THE MILKING." THAT MEANS THAT PEOPLE IN WISCONSIN ARE HARD WORKERS. IN THE EARLY DAYS, PEOPLE FROM SEVERAL DIFFERENT COUNTRIES MOVED TO WISCONSIN BECAUSE OF ITS PLENTIFUL AND RICH FARMLAND.

Today, people from many cultures still work together in Wisconsin. More than 42 percent of the population is of German descent. Wisconsin is one of the most German-American states in the country. People celebrate their German heritage with festivals such as Oktoberfest. Some people attend church services where only German is spoken.

Other ethnic groups that settled in Wisconsin also continue to honor their traditions. The city of New Glarus in southern Wisconsin is called "Little Switzerland" because of its Swiss background. Not far from Madison is Little Norway, an authentic old-world Norwegian-looking village. Today, Wisconsinites can travel Wisconsin's Ethnic Settlement Trail and tour the sites where their ancestors first settled.

Amidst the Wisconsin farmland (opposite) is the community of Little Norway, with structures such as the Norway Building (above).

YEAR
1871
More than 1,200 people die in the Great Peshtigo Fire that rages through northeastern Wisconsin's forests.
EVENT

The populations of many ethnic groups in Wisconsin are growing. About six percent of Wisconsin's residents are African American. Another five percent of the population is Hispanic, and two percent of Wisconsin's people are Asian American. About 25,000 American Indians still live in Wisconsin. Most of them live on the Menominee reservation, an area of land set aside for Indians in northeastern Wisconsin.

Most Wisconsinites live in the eastern part of the state. This is where the first settlers lived. Today, 68 percent of Wisconsin's people live in cities there. Many live in Milwaukee, the state's largest city. Milwaukee is near the southeastern corner of the state on the edge of Lake Michigan. Many other people live in Madison, the state capital.

The nearly 100-year-old state capitol in Madison (opposite) rivals the modern-looking Milwaukee Art Museum (above).

YEAR

1884 The Ringling brothers start their famous circus in the central Wisconsin city of Baraboo.

EVENT

Do Spirits Return?

HOUDINI

SAYS NO - AND PROVES IT
3 SHOWS IN ONE
MAGIC-ILLUSIONS-ESCAPES = FRAUD MEDIUMS EXPOSED

LYCEUM THEATRE
PATERSON
THURS. FRI. SAT. SEPT. 2·3·4
MATINEE SATURDAY

Wisconsin residents work in many different industries. The state ranks first in the country in the production of paper products. A 39-mile (63 km) stretch of land along the Fox River from Lake Winnebago to Green Bay has 24 paper mills. Some Wisconsinites work in Appleton to make paper bags. People in Madison make hot dogs at the Oscar Mayer meat plant. Other workers make overalls and matches in Oshkosh. The logging and cranberry industries are big business. And of course, many Wisconsinites work in the dairy industry.

Throughout its history, Wisconsin has been the home of many notable people. Harry Houdini grew up in Appleton in the 1870s and became a famous magician. Houdini amazed people with his tricks. He could free himself from handcuffs and escape from boxes under water. When Houdini went to a town to perform, he would first lock himself in jail. Within minutes, he would walk free.

Harry Houdini (pictured in a poster for his magic show, opposite) and the Oscar Mayer Wienermobile are icons of Wisconsin's history.

YEAR

1917 The first radio station in America is launched at the University of Wisconsin–Madison.

EVENT

A well-known architect named Frank Lloyd Wright was born in 1867 in the southwestern town of Richland Center. Wright did not like small, box-like houses. He designed Prairie Style homes that blended in with the landscape around them. The homes had wide-open living spaces with central fireplaces. Wright built hundreds of homes, banks, and churches in Wisconsin and throughout the U.S.

Author Laura Ingalls Wilder was born in Pepin in 1867. She is most famous for her "Little House on the Prairie" series of books. Another famous woman, Golda Meir, lived in Milwaukee in the early 1900s. She became a teacher in the city. Meir went on to become the country of Israel's first woman prime minister.

The houses created by Frank Lloyd Wright (opposite) were much more spacious than the log cabin home of Laura Ingalls Wilder (above) but were made to look as naturally simple.

1932   Wisconsin passes the first law in the U.S. that gives money to help unemployed people live.

Vacationland

MANY PEOPLE TRAVEL TO WISCONSIN FOR OUTDOOR
FUN. EVERY WINTER, MORE THAN 7,000 CROSS-COUNTRY
SKIERS GATHER AT TELEMARK RESORT NEAR CABLE,
WISCONSIN. THEY COME TO RACE IN THE AMERICAN
BIRKEBEINER. THE 31-MILE (50 KM) RACE WINDS SOUTH
THROUGH THE WOODS OF NORTHWESTERN WISCONSIN
AND FINISHES ON HAYWARD'S MAIN STREET. THE RACE,

Caves on the Apostle Islands are even more spectacular when covered in ice.

fondly called "the Birkie," was started in 1973 by resort owner Tony Wise. He patterned it after a Norwegian ski marathon. Long ago, Norwegian soldiers were called "Birkebeiners" because they strapped on birchbark leggings when they skied. Today, skiers come from all over the world to compete in Wisconsin's Birkebeiner. Kids from ages 10 to 18 can ski in the Junior Birkie.

Wisconsinites can also enjoy downhill skiing at any of the state's 50 ski resorts. Most of the resorts are in the northern part of the state where few people live. Snowmobile drivers also zip along the snowy, scenic trails. The Snowmobile Hall of Fame & Museum is located in St. Germain.

Other features of the north are the Apostle Islands of Lake Superior. Visitors can ride a ferry from Bayfield out to the islands. The 22 islands have unique rock formations, caves, and rose-colored cliffs. Six lighthouses shine over the lake and wilderness areas. Visitors paddle, sail, and cruise around these Lake Superior island jewels.

Hearty skiers brave the cold temperatures for a chance to race in the American Birkebeiner.

YEAR
1967
EVENT
The Green Bay Packers win the first-ever Super Bowl, and the next year they win Super Bowl II.

The Ducks were first built during World War II for military use, but they now carry tourists.

The Wisconsin Dells is another unique vacation destination. The Dells are found on both sides of the Wisconsin River in south-central Wisconsin. Visitors to the Dells take tours on old military land/water vehicles called Ducks. Ducks carry tourists along wooded trails. Then visitors experience exciting "splash-downs" as the Ducks enter the Wisconsin River. As boats, the Ducks pass sandstone cliffs and strange rock formations with even stranger names—such as Fat Man's Misery, Devil's Elbow, and Witches' Gulch. The narrow squeeze through Red Bird Gorge is especially thrilling.

Wisconsin's Door County is also a popular tourist attraction. The thumb-shaped peninsula juts out into Lake Michigan. Visitors can watch wooden boats being built in Sturgeon Bay. They can also feast on a traditional Door County fish boil. Potatoes, onions, and a basket of whitefish are cooked in a kettle over a hot, wood fire. When the steamy water boils over the top, the meal is ready. For dessert, people sample sweet, Door County cherry pie.

While visiting Door County, some people stop in Green Bay at the Green Bay Packers' Football Hall of Fame. Because of the state's dairy industry, Packers fans are nicknamed "Cheeseheads." Wisconsinites proudly wear "cheesehead hats" to Packers games.

Snow often falls during late-season games at the Green Bay Packers' Lambeau Field.

YEAR

1996 Shirley Abrahamson becomes the first woman chief justice of the Wisconsin Supreme Court.

EVENT

QUICK FACTS

Population: 5,601,640

Largest city: Milwaukee (pop. 602,191)

Capital: Madison

Entered the union: May 29, 1848

Nickname: Badger State

State flower: wood violet

State bird: robin

Size: 65,498 sq mi (169,639 sq km)—23rd-biggest in U.S.

Major industries: dairy products, farming, paper manufacturing, tourism

The Packers play home games at Lambeau Field. Earl L. "Curly" Lambeau founded and coached the Green Bay Packers and helped start the National Football League. The state's four other professional sports teams are based in the city of Milwaukee: the Brewers (baseball), Bucks (basketball), Admirals (hockey), and the Wave (soccer).

Wisconsin is a land of outdoor recreation and beautiful scenery. It is an agricultural center with cows, cranberries, and apple orchards. People visit the Badger State to ski, ice fish, and cruise in boats. More and more businesses and people are taking a closer look at the quality of life in Wisconsin. They want to find out why living in Wisconsin is so good!

BIBLIOGRAPHY

American Birkebeiner Ski Foundation. "About Us." American Birkebeiner. http://www.birkie.com/?page=1052.

Bie, Michael. *It Happened in Wisconsin*. Guilford, Conn.: Twodot Publishing, 2007.

Current, Richard. *Wisconsin: A History*. Urbana, Ill.: University of Illinois Press, 2001.

Hintz, Martin. *Hiking Wisconsin*. Champaign, Ill.: Human Kinetics Publishers, 1997.

Risjord, Norman. *Wisconsin: The Story of the Badger State*. Black Earth, Wisc.: Trails Books, 1995.

INDEX